Money

and What to Do With It!!

by Jarrod and Melissa Welsh

Illustrated by Erin Peterson

What is Money?

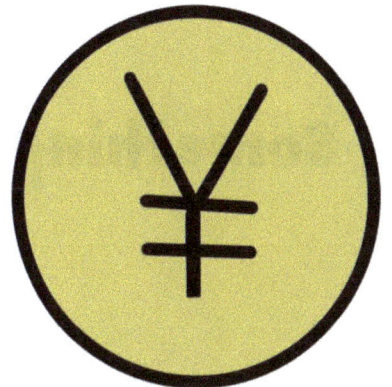

Money is:

something generally accepted as
a medium of exchange,
a measure of value,
or a means of payment

OR

Something you use to get something else!!

to do this we use

coins. . .

...and
bills

Let's learn the different kinds of **money** used in the United States

First, we'll talk about

coins

Penny

Dime

Nickel

Quarter

The first coin is the

Penny

It is worth
1 cent
or
1 hundredth of a dollar
And...

100 Pennies = 1 Dollar

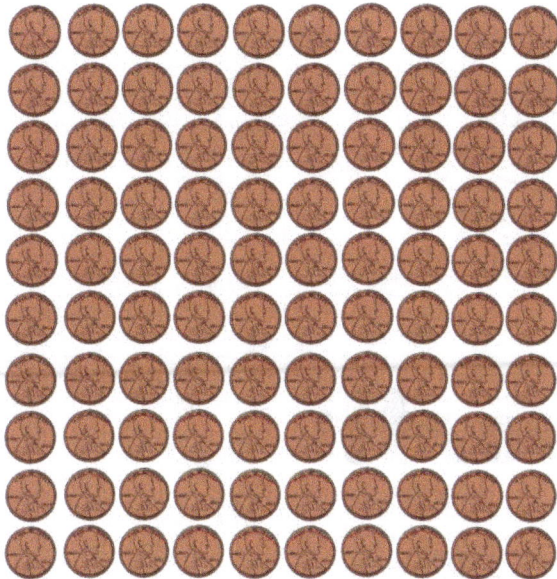

The second coin is the
Nickel

It is worth
5 cents
or
5 hundredths of a dollar
And...

20 nickels = 1 dollar

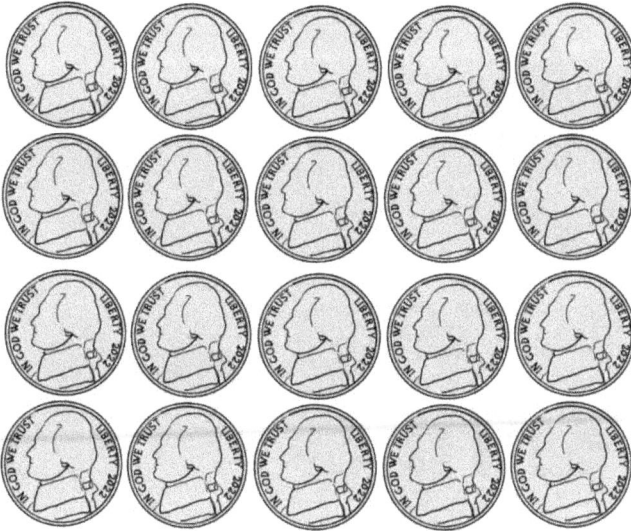 =

The Third coin is the

Dime

It is worth
10 cents
or
one tenth of a dollar
And...

10 dimes = 1 dollar

 =

The Fourth coin is the
Quarter

It is worth
25 cents
or
one fourth (or "quarter") of a dollar
And...

4 quarters = 1 dollar

 =

Next, we'll talk about

bills

The first bill is the

One Dollar Bill

THE UNITED STATES OF AMERICA

ONE DOLLAR

It is worth

1 dollar

100 Pennies

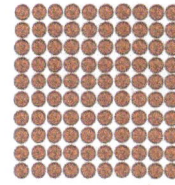

20 Nickels

1 Dollar

=

10 Dimes

4 Quarters

The Second bill is the
Five Dollar Bill

It is worth
5 dollars

5 Dollars = 5 One Dollar Bills

The Third bill is the
Ten Dollar bill

It is worth
10 dollars

10 Dollars = 10 One Dollar Bills

 =

The Fourth bill is the
Twenty Dollar bill

It is worth
20 dollars

20 Dollars = 20 One Dollar Bills

The Fifth bill is the Fifty Dollar bill

It is worth 50 dollars

50 Dollars = 50 One Dollar Bills

 =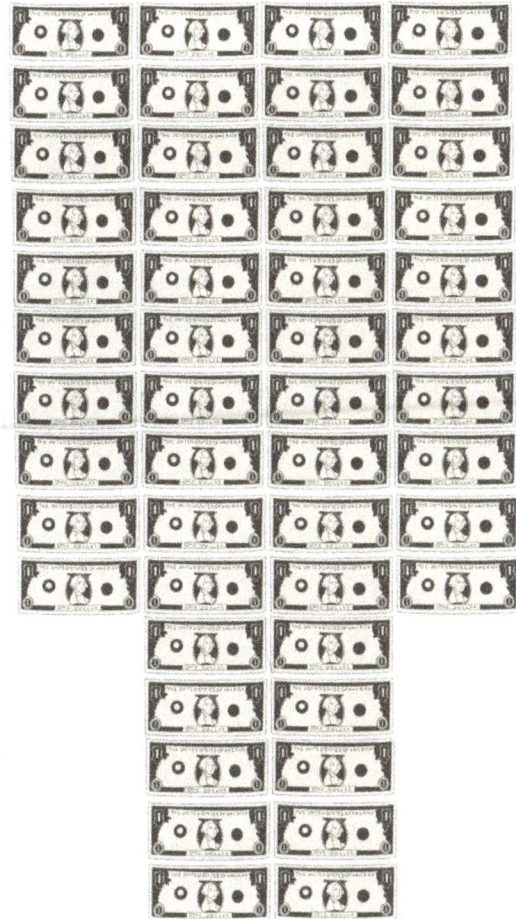

The sixth bill is the
One Hundred Dollar Bill

It is worth
100 dollars

100 Dollars = 100 One Dollar Bills

Now that we know what kind of money there is...

...let's talk about what you can do with it!

There are four main things you can do with money

Saving   Spending

Investing   Giving

Saving

Save money for the *future.*

Always Pay Yourself

First

Which means:
When you get money,
always put some of it
in your

savings

before you spend it on
anything else.

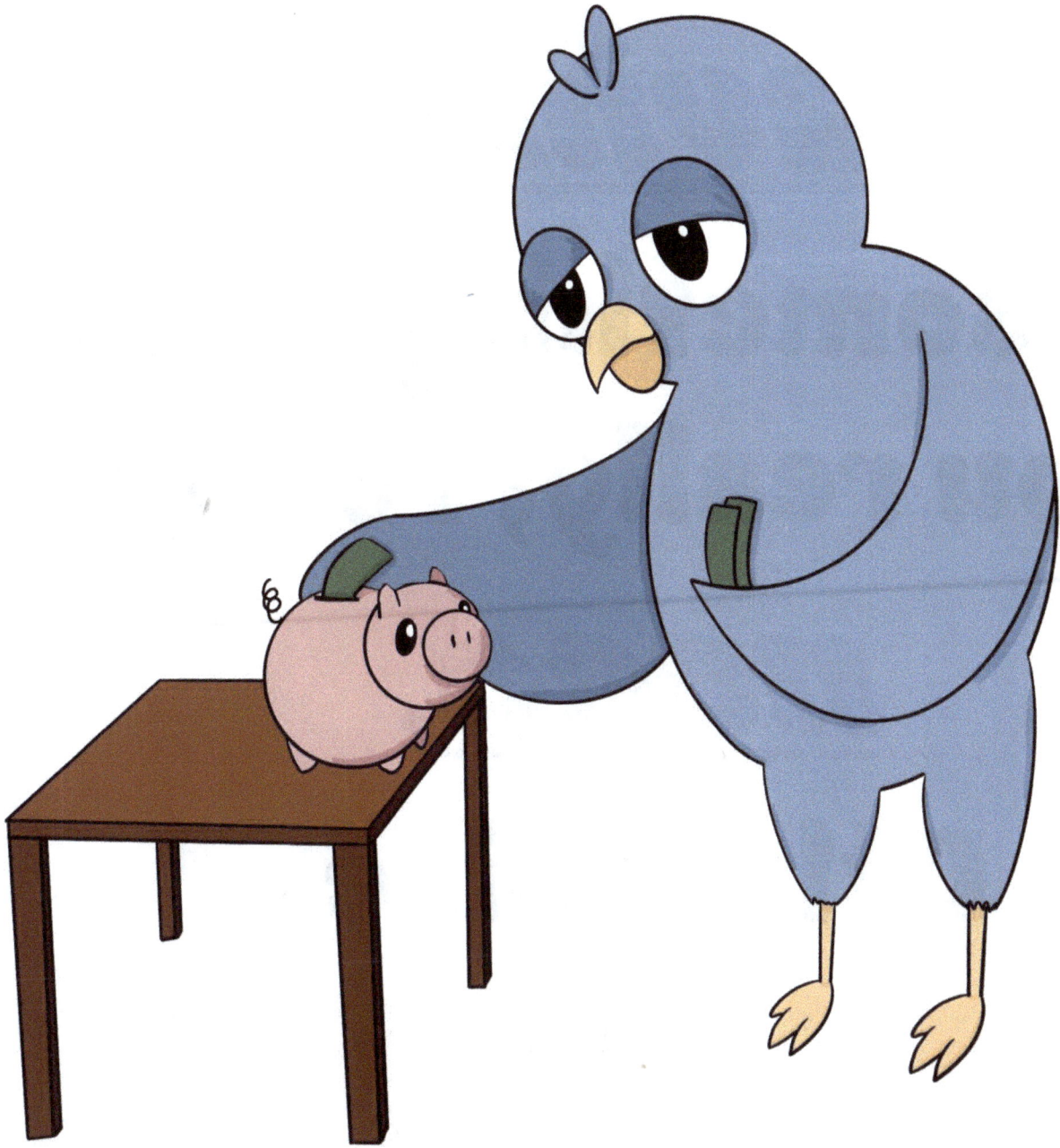

Only use your *savings* on something that you really, really *need*. Otherwise, DON'T TOUCH IT!!

You can save your your money at home

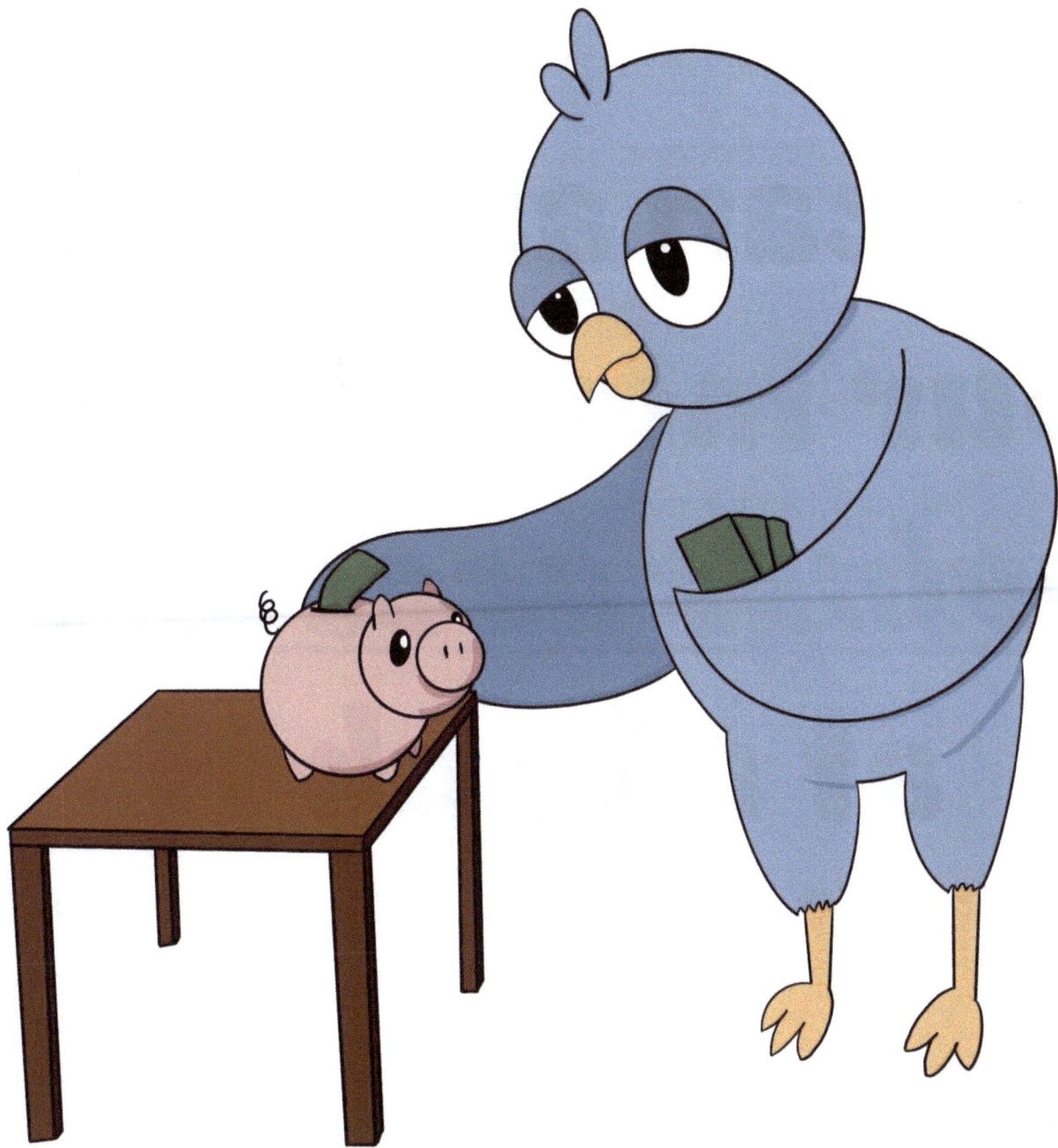

You can also put your *money* in a *savings account* at a bank

In a bank your money will earn " *interest* "

Interest

is another name for extra money the bank pays you for letting them use it!

Spending

Using money to pay people you *owe* AND to buy things you *need to live* (food, water, shelter) AND things that you *want*

Spending your money can be fun, but you must do it wisely

When you owe **money**, it is called a *debt*.
If you have any *debts*, you must pay them before buying the things you *want*.

Your goal should be to have very few or no debts.

Being *debt-free* allows you to save, spend, invest, and give more of your money!!

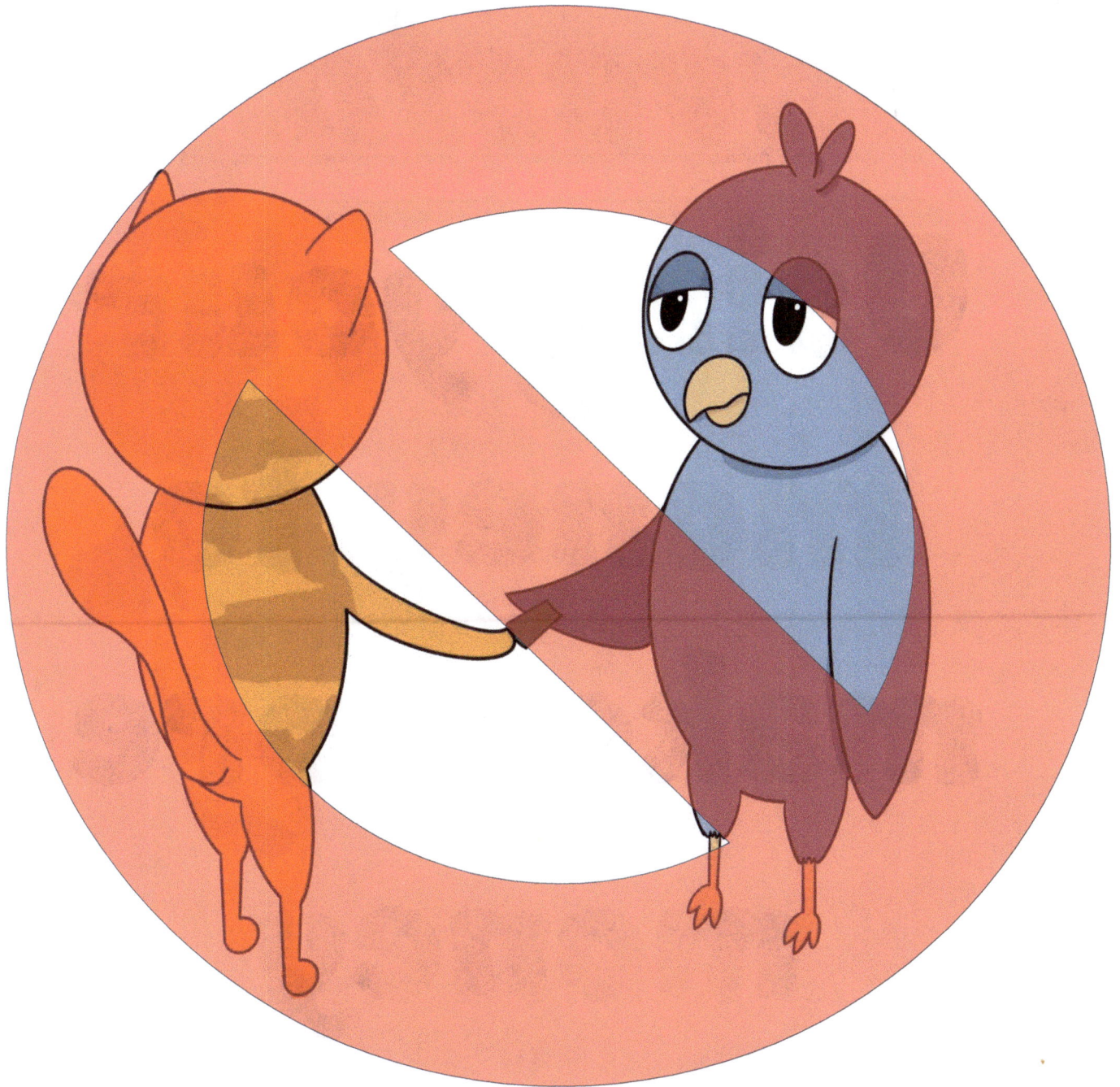

Investing

Using your money to make more money

Investing

your money is

smart

and will make your money grow into more money!

You can *invest* in *stocks* which means you own part of a *company* or *business*

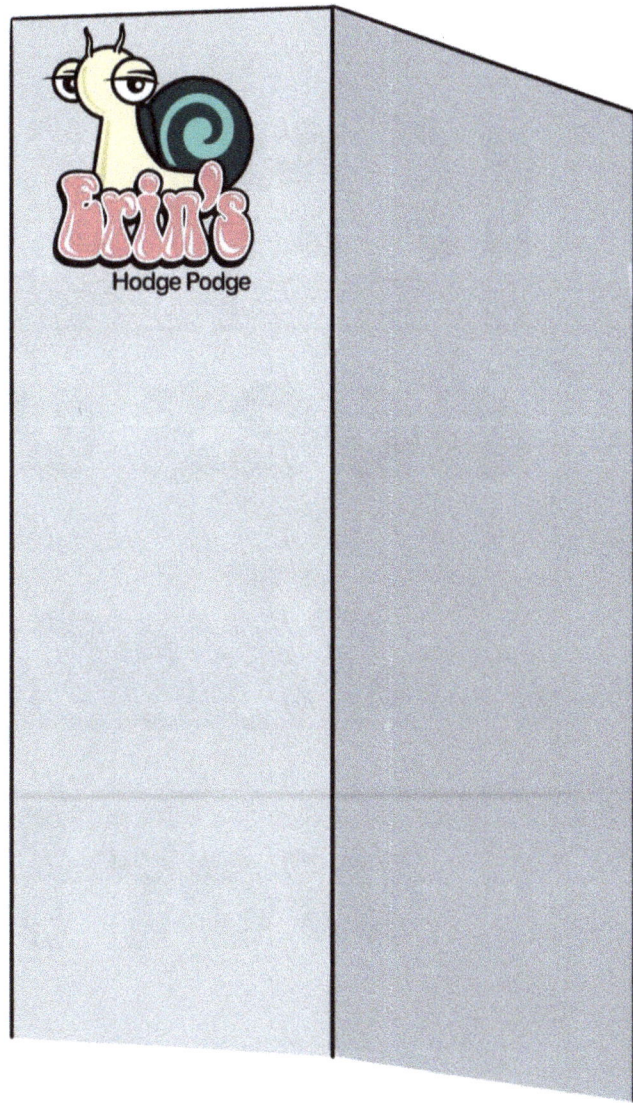

If the *company* does well, your *stock* will be worth more money!

You can also *invest* in real estate which is a fancy way to say buying buildings

Then, people will pay you money to use your new buildings!

You can also *invest* your money into savings bonds

A *bond* is money the government or a company *borrows* from you

Then,
after some time,
the government
or company gives
you back your

money

plus,
even more!

Caution!

Bonds from the government are much safer than **_bonds_** from a private company!

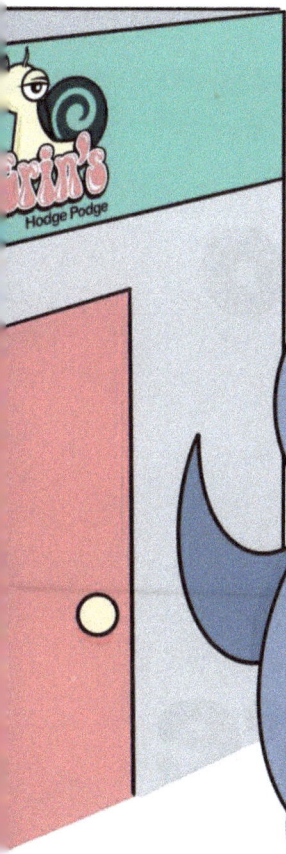

Giving

Give money to help

others who are not as fortunate as you

Giving your money to *charity* is nice and helps others get the things they *need*.

So, when you earn money, don't spend it all right away!

Save
it first...

...then buy the things you *need to live* (food, water, shelter)

...then *pay* the people you *owe* (*debts*)...

...then

invest

some...

...then *help* someone in need by *giving* them some of your money...

...then *buy* the things you *want* with the rest!!

That is money
and what to do with it!

Be smart with your money to have a successful and happy life!!

The End!!

For other books in the *Children's Life Toolkit* series, aim your camera here for:
I'm In Control!!

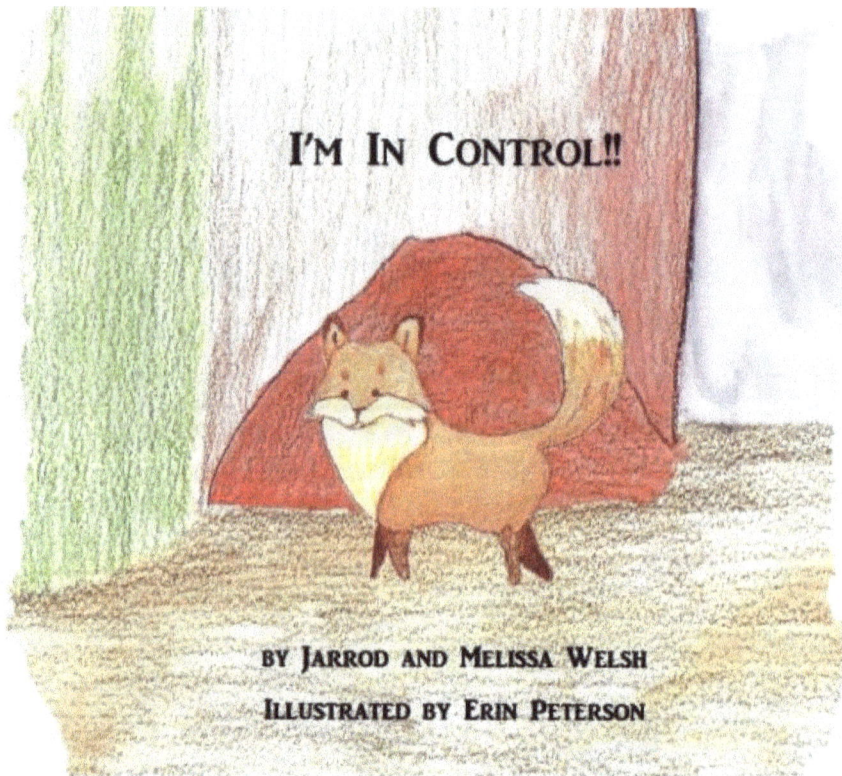

I'M IN CONTROL!!

BY JARROD AND MELISSA WELSH

ILLUSTRATED BY ERIN PETERSON

...and here for:

Words Can't Hurt Me!

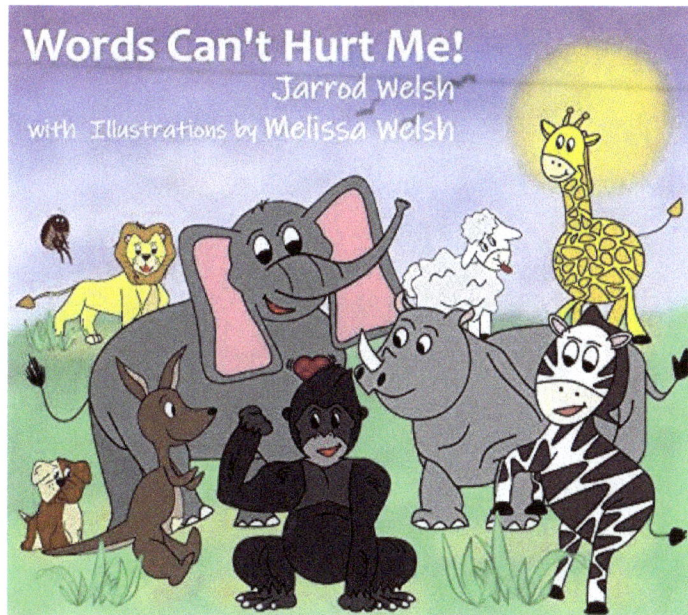

...and here for:

Happiness Will Come, You'll See!

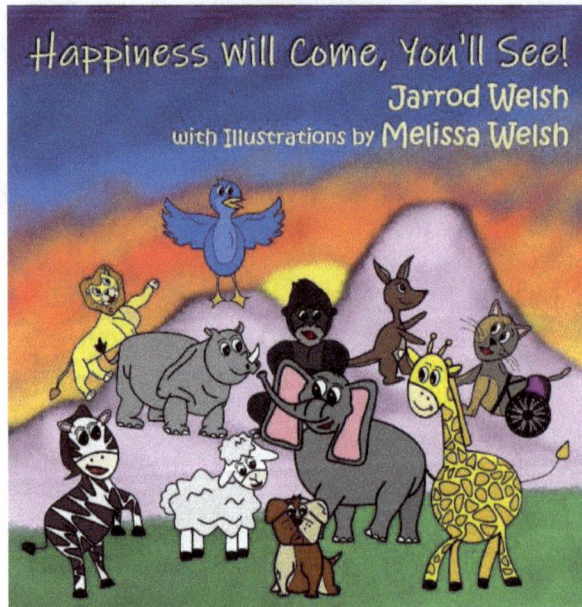

Happiness Will Come, You'll See!

Jarrod Welsh

with Illustrations by Melissa Welsh

...and here for two in one!

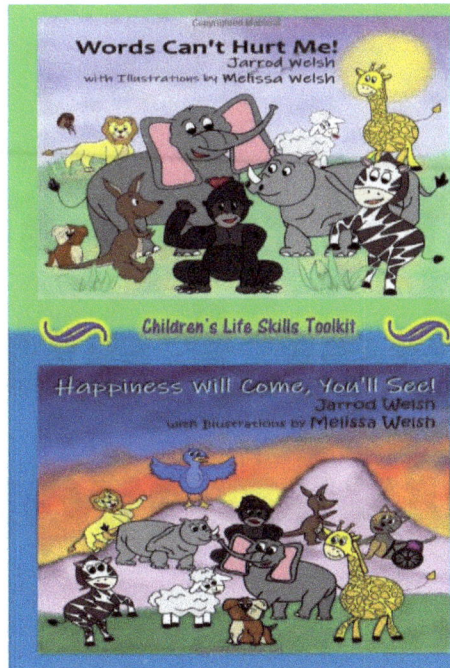

Go here:

Etsy

to find out more about our illustrator!!

Contact Info:

Jarrod@tryitlikethis.net

www.ingramcontent.com/pod-product-compliance
Lightning Source LLC
Chambersburg PA
CBHW062106090426
42741CB00015B/3337